# *Baptism*

## THE MOST PRECIOUS GIFT

### Complete Manual for Parent Preparation

*Beth Branigan McNamara*

Our Sunday Visitor Publishing Division
Our Sunday Visitor, Inc.
Huntington, IN 46750

*Nihil Obstat*
Rev. John M. Kuzmich

*Imprimatur*
✠ John M. D'Arcy
Bishop of Fort Wayne-South Bend
March 28, 1996

# Table of Contents

## Supplements

# Introduction

*"All power in heaven and on earth has been given to me. Go, therefore, and make disciples of all nations, baptizing them in the name of the Father, and of the Son, and of the holy Spirit, teaching them to observe all that I have commanded you. And behold, I am with you always, until the end of the age" (Matthew 28:19-20).*

Baptism is truly the most precious gift children receive as they come into the world to begin their life's journey. Baptism initiates us into: the life of the Spirit, union with Christ, and membership in the Church. As a Catholic community we are called to evangelize and through Baptism to make disciples of Christ. Baptism is at the heart of who we are as a Catholic community.

As the Apostle Paul indicated, through Baptism children are brought into communion with Christ's death, are buried, and rise with him (Romans 6:3-4). As members of the Body of Christ, the parents profess their commitment to make a home where the gospel is lived, the godparents and all members of the community promise to support the parents in this. This is a serious covenant into which we enter.

This is the perfect time for these parents to have the opportunity to share their thoughts, reaffirm their own baptismal commitment, and deepen their faith. The life of faith means having a personal relationship with Christ through grace, which is nurtured by God's Word and the sacramental life of the Church.

The new *Catechism* reminds us that, "The faith required for Baptism is not a perfect and mature faith, but a beginning that is called to develop " (CCC 1253). Baptism calls us to continual conversion. Young children will not understand this, but their parents can understand and strive to live a life that reflects their faith and values. Our Catholic community has a responsibility to parents and children to support and aid them in their spiritual growth and formation prior to Baptism and beyond.

*Baptism, the Most Precious Gift* is a Baptism preparation program that deepens the parents' understanding of Baptism and their ongoing conversion. Led by faith-filled members of your church community, parents (and godparents) are given guidance and support as they begin to raise their child in the Catholic faith. Everything needed to do this is in this manual.

### The Baptism preparation sessions

The manual contains three complete, easy-to-use baptism preparation sessions. For each session you will find a reproducible parent booklet and insert that include prayer, scripture, reflection, and helpful information about the sacrament. Simple, step-by-step instructions will lead you through each session. The sessions are easily adapted to fit your parish needs.

Each session is approximately two hours long and can be comfortably facilitated by an individual or a team of people. The participants will respond to the thought-provoking questions, interesting activities, and input given by team members. Fit your parish needs by using all three or a combination of the sessions. The third session can easily be used as a follow-up after the celebration of Baptism.

### Individual or team leadership

The number of people you have on the baptism preparation team will depend on the size of your parish. Whether the preparation is led by an individual or a group of volunteers, the leadership is an important asset to your program. In the section titled "Baptism leadership" you will find help with recruiting, training, and care of these people.

The leadership training outline is very flexible and can be used as one two-hour session or broken up into two one-hour sessions. If you lead the preparation alone in your parish, simply read through the training to get an overview of the sessions.

## Resources

### Blackline masters

Everything you need for all three of the parent preparation sessions, from the welcome letter and information form to the parent booklets and evaluations, are found on reproducible blackline masters. Your preparation and celebration will be enhanced with Baptism candle decorating ideas, a letter for the godparents explaining their ongoing role, and a Baptism certificate, all found on the blackline masters in the back of the book.

### Supplements

This section provides an extensive assortment of resources including bulletin announcements, clip art, and tips that will help team members facilitate the sessions and make presentations.

All you need to implement this program is a small group of faith-filled parish members and a copy machine.

*Note: The marked components are found in the "Resources" section of this manual.*

### Getting started

Familiarize yourself with the manual and the three complete sessions provided.

Each session consists of these main elements:
- Welcome
- Climate setting
- Overview
- Opening prayer
- Presentation of information (content varies from session to session)
- Discussion and input activities
- Reflection of personal faith
- Closing prayer/blessing

### Program organization

#### Identify team members

Read through "Baptism leadership" (page 8) to understand the characteristics and qualities needed in the baptismal preparation team. Use the volunteer interest letter (page 25) to send to identified possible program volunteers.

#### Set dates

As soon as possible, provide priest/deacon and other program members involved with the dates for team training, parent sessions, and celebration of Baptisms. Confirm these dates with a follow-up phone call or letter.

#### Reserve meeting space

Meeting space should be a comfortable, small-group setting where simple refreshments can be served.

#### Conduct training

Use "Training for the Baptism leadership" (page 9) to provide the volunteers with the confidence to lead the sessions comfortably. Other helpful information for leading the sessions will be found in "Tips for group discussion" and "Presentation guide" (page 60).

#### Announce program

Invite parents to register for the Baptism preparation sessions by publishing a bulletin announcement (page 59) of upcoming sessions. Using clip art (page 47) draws attention to the notice.

#### Send welcome letters

The note of welcome (page 29) will warmly greet and provide registered parents with needed information for the upcoming session.

#### Delegate responsibilities

Meet with the team or phone each of the members to delegate the responsibilities for the sessions including welcoming, refreshments, presentations, etc.

#### Conduct Baptism preparation sessions

- Session one — theology and history
- Session two — symbols, godparents, and ritual
- Session three — Catholic family and parish life

These sessions may be conducted in one of three manners:

- All three sessions are presented consecutively prior to the child's celebration of the sacrament.
- The first two sessions presented before the child celebrates the sacrament, with the third session following the Baptism.
- The three sessions are easily adapted to meet the specific needs of your parish. You could combine sessions 1 and 2 or sessions 2 and 3. Simply write the objectives you want to meet on a planning sheet. Individualize the session by pulling topics, prayers, and activities from the three sessions offered in this manual. The participant booklets are easily pieced together to conform to any newly devised sessions.

#### Evaluate

At the end of each session make available a follow-up sheet to allow volunteers to share their insights (page 51). During the final session provide a program evaluation form for the participants to complete (page 52).

#### Announce celebration of Baptisms

Invite the community to participate in the celebration of the sacrament by publicizing the dates, times, and names of those to be baptized. Notice can be included in the church bulletin or on a board in the church entrance or gathering space.

### Celebrate Baptisms

Collect the needed information before the celebration using the "Baptism information" sheet (page 49). Offer the "Record of Baptism" (page 57) as a remembrance of this special day. Give the "Godparent booklet" (page 55) to the godparents to remind them of their important role and responsibilities to the child and the family.

### Announce newly baptized

Congratulate the newly baptized in the bulletin the week after the celebration.

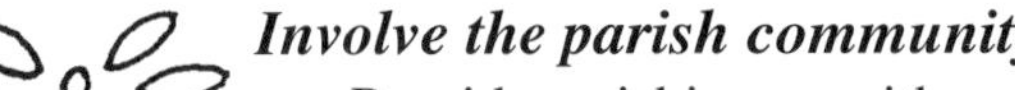

### Involve the parish community

Provide parishioners with opportunities to become involved in the celebration and preparation of Baptism. Some ideas:

- Invite members to make *white garments* to be used in the rite.
- Seek out groups to help organize materials such as assembling the Baptism candle kits.
- Ask the community to pray for the newly baptized and their families.

# Scope and Sequence



When a parent comes to the Church requesting the sacrament of Baptism for a child, the community helps the parent prepare through a process of prayer, reflection, and exploration:

**Theology**: The theology of Baptism is the foundation upon which the preparation builds.

**History**: The history of Baptism helps further our understanding of the meaning of the sacrament.

**Symbols and godparents**: As the history is traced the symbols and their significance in our lives become clear.

**Rite**: The rite of Baptism reflects the theology, history, and symbols of this sacrament of initiation.

**Catholic family life**: The parents, with the help and support of the godparents and community, promise to model and teach the values and beliefs of the Catholic faith to their child.

**Parish life**: The Catholic community invites the active participation of the parents and the child in the life of the community.

**Deepened Catholic faith**: As the parents (godparents) prepare for the child's baptism, their faith deepens as does their understanding of the Catholic community.

# Baptism leadership

## Leadership functions:

- Welcomes parents and families who are having their child baptized
- Acts as group facilitators
- Helps with setup, process, presentation, and cleanup of the sessions
- Shares their personal faith and experiences living as members of Catholic families

## Team characteristics:

- Reflects the diversity of the parish
- "Empty nest" parents
- Parents of toddlers
- Parents of teenagers
- Single parents
- Interfaith marriages
- Exhibits a balance of men, women, young, and old (as much as possible)

## Individual characteristics:

- Spiritually mature, faith-filled Catholic
- Good listening skills
- Willingness to share and communicate their faith
- Genuine sense of welcome

## Recruitment tips

*Look for members year 'round.* Waiting until an unexpected vacancy arises may present a problem. Always encourage new inquiries about volunteering for the baptismal program. Parents attending the sessions may possess just the qualities the team needs to present a balance.

*Point out the advantages for participating in this ministry.* Each individual will value different reasons for serving on the Baptism team:

- Taking an active role in the church community
- Living out a commitment to Christian families
- Developing personal faith to grow as it is shared with others
- Supporting other families on their faith journey

*Be clear and concise when defining the member's role and time commitment to this ministry.* Establish definite terms for serving in the program. At the end of the term provide some form of evaluation allowing volunteers the opportunity to assess their participation in the program.

*Encourage potential members to participate before committing to the ministry.* Invite potential members to sit in when a regular member is not available. This will allow the coordinator to assess the gifts and talents of the person showing interest in this ministry.

## Training

*(see "Training for the Baptism leadership," page 9)*

## Support and growth

Provide continuous support and growth for team members throughout the year.

*Keep in touch with the volunteers* through phone calls, notes, reminder postcards, newsletters, etc.

*Show appreciation with small tokens or gifts at different seasons during the year.* These might be an ornament or candle with a prayer or scripture attached at Christmas, a bouquet of fresh-cut flowers at Easter, anything to convey the message of appreciation for that season.

*Gather the team for a celebration of their ministry a few times a year.* Acknowledge their commitment to Christian family life by including their family members at some of the events and providing child care at others. Encourage their spiritual growth by incorporating prayer and reflection in the gathering. Some suggestions for these gatherings: a potluck dinner, picnic, volleyball game, etc.

## Evaluate

Provide the team members the opportunity to evaluate the program and their participation (see page 51).

# *Training for the Baptism leadership*

*Note: The ideal training for team members would be to participate in the three baptismal preparation sessions prior to joining the team. If time permits, this two-hour training could easily be adapted to be done in two one-hour sessions.*

## Training session overview

### Objectives

- To familiarize the team with the process used in the sessions while building confidence and enthusiasm for the program
- To build community among team members

### Preparation

- Copy and collate the participant booklets titled "Loved by God, Marked With the Sign of the Cross" (see page 37).
- Copy and cut apart one set of history cards (see page 35).
- Fill a pocket folder with the following items for each team member: nametags, phone list of team members, notebook, pen or pencil, team manual.

### Materials

- Refreshments
- Team folders
- Newsprint pad (found at any school/office supply store)
- Markers

### Process

- Welcome
- Climate setting
- Overview
- Opening prayer
- Discussion and input from session one
- Break
- Discussion and input from sessions two and three
- Reflection of personal faith
- Blessing

---

## The training session

### Welcome

Warmly greet volunteers as they enter the room. Ask them to take the following:

- Nametag
- Team member folder
- Refreshments

Thank everyone for coming together for this training. Introduce the team members.

### Climate setting

Use one of the icebreakers from Baptism preparation session one to help people relax and become better acquainted with one another.

### Reflection

1) Give the team members a few moments to quietly reflect on the following statement: *Why did you choose to become a Baptism team member?*

2) Ask that they record their reflections in the notebook provided.

3) Inform the members that they will be invited to share their thoughts as the conclusion of the opening prayer.

### Overview

The church community wants to support families requesting baptism for their children. This baptismal preparation team acts on behalf of the church to support, guide, and welcome these families. The same process used in this training session will be used during all three of the Baptism preparation sessions.

1) Ask the group members to locate the "process" section for sessions one, two, and three in their team manuals.

2) Point out that each session's process follows a similar sequence.

3) Ask the group to identify this sequence and record the steps on the newsprint:

Welcome
Climate setting
Overview
Opening prayer
Reflection/discussion/input
Break
Reflection/discussion/input
Reflection of personal faith
Review of the next session (sessions one and two)
Blessing

4) As you go through the sessions, from time to time point to the newsprint to indicate where in the process sequence the group is working.

### Opening prayer

1) Each baptismal preparation session of this program begins with an opening prayer found on pages 1 and 2 of each session's participant booklet.

2) While pointing this out, hand out participant booklet two, titled "Loved by God, Marked With the Sign of the Cross." Draw the member's attention to the opening prayer found on the cover.

3) To familiarize the group with the opening prayer:
• Select a leader to read Ephesians 4:4-6.
• Point out the response at the bottom of the booklet cover.
• Invite everyone to pray aloud the "Our Father" found at the top of page 2 in participant booklet two.
• Remind the group that they will be invited to share their recorded reflections.

4) Before you begin the prayer invite the group to sit quietly for a moment, recognizing God's presence and his powerful love for each person present.

5) Pray:

**Leader**: Baptism is a sacrament of faith. Faith is lived out in a community of believers, the Body of Christ. As the *Catechism of the Catholic Church* reminds us, "The faith required for Baptism is not a perfect and mature faith" (1253), but a beginning from which God calls us to grow and deepen. The parents and godparents are asked: "What do you ask of God's Church?" The response is "Faith!" (CCC 1253)

**Reader**: A reading from Ephesians 4:4-6:

"There is but one body and one Spirit, just as there is but one hope given to all of you by your call. There is one Lord, one faith, one baptism; one God and Father of all, who is over all, and works through all, and is in all."

**Response**: We have been called by God and to God we belong.

**Leader**: Together let us pray a prayer that unifies Christians as does Baptism.

**All**: Our Father, who art in heaven, hallowed be thy name. Thy kingdom come. Thy will be done on earth, as it is in heaven. Give us this day our daily bread. And forgive us our trespasses, as we forgive those who trespass against us. And lead us not into temptation, but deliver us from evil. Amen.

#### Shared Reflection:

Why did you choose to become a Baptism team member?

Express your appreciation for their willingness to share in this important ministry.

### Discussion and input

1) Ask everyone to turn to the resource pages for session one.

2) Lead the group through the session one process, highlighting the resource pages in the discussion.

3) When the discussion reaches the history section have the group use the "fact discovery" cards to ask and answer a few questions. The cards will piece together a brief history of Baptism.

4) Continue the discussion until session one is completed.

### Break

Invite everyone to:
• Get up and stretch
• Refill their refreshments
• Share some conversation

### Discussion and input

After calling the group back from the break, continue the discussion in the same manner as for session one, except that you will use activities from sessions two and three. Choose activities from the following:

***Session two***
• Reflection — "Symbols that reveal the richness and meaning of Baptism"
or
• Visit the church for the ritual of Baptism.

***Session three***
• Christian Family Life activity

### Reflection of personal faith

Use the personal faith reflection from either session one or two.

### Blessing

1) Invite the members to focus on the blessing found on page 4 of the participant booklet from session two pointing out that each session will conclude with a blessing.

2) Ask the members to bow their heads and receive God's blessing taken from the "Rite of Baptism":

By God's gift, through water and the Holy Spirit, we are reborn to everlasting life.

In God's goodness, may he continue to pour out his blessings upon all present, who are God's sons and daughters.

May God make them always, wherever they may be, faithful members of his holy people.
May God send peace to all who are gathered here, in Christ Jesus our Lord.
**All**: Amen (paraphrased from the "Rite of Baptism").

### Final notes

Invite the group members to take a team manual home and go through it. Encourage members to jot down any questions they might have and to keep in touch with you.

*For your notes ...*

# *Promised and Made New in Baptism*

## Session one overview

### *Objectives*

- To give parents the opportunity to think about and discuss their understanding of Baptism.
- To see Baptism as a sacrament of initiation, the first step in Christian formation, made with other members of the Church.
- To give an overview of the history of the sacrament in order to understand and appreciate the importance and joyful reality of Baptism.
- To help parents begin to look at their own faith life and the faith that they will share with their child.

### *Preparation*

- Be prepared to present "Baptism is rich in meaning" (see page 13).
- Copy back to back and fold to make participant booklet "Promised and Made New in Baptism" (see page 31).
- Copy back to back on half sheets to make insert "You Are Chosen" (see page 33).
- Copy one set of history question and answer cards back to back and cut apart (see page 35).

### *Materials*

- Nametags
- Pens
- Refreshments
- Set of history fact cards
- Participant booklets titled "Promised and Made New"
- Booklet insert titled "You Are Chosen"
- Newsprint
- Markers

### *Process*

- Welcome
- Climate setting
- Overview
- Opening prayer
- Reflection, "Reasons for Baptism" discussion and input of Baptism theology
- Break
- History of Baptism "fact discovery"
- Reflection of personal faith
- Overview of next session
- Closing prayer and blessing

---

## Session one

### *Welcome*

1) Welcome parents as they arrive.

2) Invite the parents to:
  - Fill out a nametag
  - Take a "Promised and Made New" booklet to look through
  - Complete the statement at the top of page 2
  - Get some refreshments

3) Introduce the members of the team. As representatives of the parish, warmly welcome the parents. Let them know that the parish community rejoices with them for this wonderful gift of new life.

4) Explain that the sacrament of Baptism is the most precious and important gift that they can give their child.

5) Express your appreciation for their coming and taking another step in sharing the love of God with their child.

### *Climate setting*

This will not only set the tone for the session but give people the opportunity to get to know other families in the community.

*(Note: If you have a small group of eight to ten people do this icebreaker as one group. If your group is larger, break into smaller groups following the team introductions. Be sure to give each group enough time to become acquainted.)*

1) Use one of the following icebreakers to help people relax and become acquainted:

- Invite each person to introduce him/herself, telling a little bit about him/herself and then complete one of these phrases:

  The best thing that happened to me this week was ...

  If I were not here I would be ...

- Encourage each person to describe some of the various roles they have in life — mother, father, husband, wife, coworker, etc.

- Ask each person to give a brief history of his/her membership in a church community.

- Invite the group members to say the first word that comes to mind when they hear you say a word. Possible words to use might be: baby, diaper, feeding, bottle, family, etc.

2) Conclude by saying that even though we are different people many of our experiences and aspects of our lives are similar. The waters of Baptism are truly a rebirth. They symbolize an immersion into Christ's death and arising with Him to new life. We are all one in Christ through our own Baptism, and then we are members of the Body of Christ. This is why we gather. The Catholic community is a group of people who care for one another, support one another, and have a common belief in Jesus and his message. Baptism welcomes us into the Catholic community.

### Overview

The Baptism of infants and children requires a time of reflection and exploration on the part of the parents. They are the first educators of their children in the ways of faith which will reflect the image of God to their children.

1) Explain that together you will explore and prepare for the Sacrament of Baptism.

2) Briefly present the objectives for this session.

### Opening prayer

1) Invite everyone to look at the cover and page 1 of the booklet. Familiarize the group with the opening prayer by doing the following:

- Select a leader to read Psalm 139.
- Point out the response at the bottom of the booklet cover.
- Invite everyone to read aloud the prayer on page 2 of the booklet.
- Tell the group members at the conclusion of prayer they will be asked to share their reflections to the statement on page 2 of their booklet.

2) Before you begin the prayer, invite the parents to sit quietly for a moment, recognizing the presence of God and the capacity of prayer to transform our lives.

3) Pray:

**Leader**: A reading from Psalm 139:
"Truly you have formed my inmost being
    you knit me in my mother's womb.
I give you thanks that I am fearfully, wonderfully made
My soul also you knew full well;
    nor was my frame unknown to you
When I was made in secret,
    when I was fashioned in the depths of the earth."

**Response**: Thankful are we, loving God, for this precious gift of life.

**Leader**: Together let us pray …

**All**: We are filled with awe and wonder, as we give you thanks and praise, loving God.
These new lives from your creative hands are treasures to be cherished always. As we gather here open our hearts and minds, remembering that it is through water and the word that we receive your light and life.

    Amen.

 ***Shared reflection to the statement:***
"When I heard my child was coming I felt …"

### Reflection — reasons for Baptism

1) Ask group members to open the parent booklet to page 3.

2) Allow the parents a few minutes to read through and fill out this page. Let the parents know that there are no specifically right or wrong answers. The activity is meant to help them clarify their own understanding of infant Baptism.

3) Ask if anyone would like to share his/her responses to the statements. Elicit his/her reasons for having a child baptized.

4) Invite others to do the same.

### Discussion and input

After everyone has had the opportunity to share their reasons for Baptism, give a presentation using the following outline to deepen the discussion about Baptism.

## Baptism is rich in meaning

I. Baptism is a sacrament, an encounter with Christ, a time when Christ comes to us and acts within us and among us. Thus Baptism is an event of transformation of the child, family, and community. It is a powerful and visual reminder to all the participants that God's love and salvation are not earned but offered to us as a gift (CCC 1282).

II. In Baptism we are freed from original sin and given a share in the life of grace (CCC 1279). Original sin is a condition of separation from God and of our personal weakness in living as God's people. Original sin is removed when we are filled with the love and grace of Christ. Grace is the experience of God's loving and empowering presence in our lives.

III. Thus Baptism is the beginning of a new life in Christ and the Church (CCC 1277). Through the life, death, and resurrection of Christ, we are awakened to the fullness that Christ brings to us in this lifetime and beyond death.

IV. The Catholic community rejoices and celebrates the child's initiation into the Body of Christ. The community welcomes the child and extends its support to the child and family in living a life that reflects Jesus to the world.

V. Responsibility for the child to know and follow Jesus and learn more about faith, is first and foremost, the parents', shared, supported, and nurtured by the godparents and the Catholic community (CCC 1255).

2) Distribute the "You Are Chosen" insert for parents to read at home.

### *Break*
Invite everyone to:
- Get up and stretch
- Refill their refreshments
- Share some conversation

## *History of Baptism*
Baptism is the oldest tradition of the Church. It reminds us of our roots in the history of God's chosen people. The history of Baptism gives us a better perspective and appreciation of the sacrament. Use the blackline master "Fact Discovery" cards to share some highlights in the long history of Baptism.
1) Give ten participants each a "Fact Discovery" card.
2) After they have had a few moments to read through the card, invite them to share the information with the group.
3) As the group goes through the information on the cards, highlight the main events on the newsprint using the provided timeline as a model.

### *Baptism timeline*

John the Baptist: first century; water Baptisms/holy spirit

Apostles are called to baptize: first century

Catechumenate: second century; white garment

Roman Empire: fourth century

Augustine's theology: fifth century; infant Baptism

Preparation for Baptism lessens: sixth century

Confirmation separate sacrament: ninth century

Vatican II Council: 1963

*Catechism of the Catholic Church*: 1994

4) Conclude this activity by saying that the Church has a long and rich history. The *Catechism of the Catholic Church* affirms Baptism as the first sacrament of initiation and the beginning of a growing personal relationship with Christ and the Catholic community.

### *Reflection of personal faith*
1) Invite the parents to turn to the last page in their booklet and find the section titled "Faith in my life."
2) Ask the parents to read and think about this section at home prior to the next session.
- Someone who has helped me grow in my faith and response to God …
- What they shared with me …

### *Overview of the next session*
Give parents a brief idea of topics to be covered at the following meeting
- Choosing godparents
- Celebration of Baptism
- The ritual and symbols
- Growing in faith

### *Closing prayer and blessing*
Invite the parents to bow their heads and receive God's blessing as the following is read aloud from page 4 of the booklet:

God the Father, through the Son, the Virgin Mary's Child, has brought joy to all Christian parents, as they see the hope of eternal life shine on their children. May God bless the parents of these children. May they be one with them in thanking God forever in heaven, in Christ Jesus our Lord.

**All**: Amen (paraphrased from the "Rite of Baptism").

### *Final notes*
1) Remind the group of the dates and times of future classes.
2) Invite the participants to stay after, if they have any questions or concerns that they would like to discuss with you.

# *Loved by God, Marked With the Sign of the Cross*

## Session two overview

### *Objectives*
- To explore and understand the depth of God's gift to us in the symbols of Baptism.
- To give the parents guidance and essential information for choosing godparents.
- To provide a preview of the Baptism ceremony, giving parents an insight into the powerful richness of the ritual.
- To continue to help parents examine their own faith life and the faith that they will profess at the Baptism of their child.

### *Preparation*
- Ask the deacon or priest who will be celebrating the Baptism to come to this session, meet the parents, and walk them through the ritual of Baptism (see page 18).
- Copy back to back and fold participant booklet "Loved by God, Marked With the Sign of the Cross" (see page 37).
- Copy insert back to back on half sheets of paper (see page 39).
- Using five sheets of newsprint, print one of the following words across the top on each — water, light, community of people, white garment, oil.
- Set out the actual baptismal symbol next to each corresponding sheet of newsprint — bowl of water, candle, picture of a group of people or the parish directory, baptismal garment, chrism.
- Be prepared to present "Signs of God's Love" (see page 17).
- Organize candle kits (see pages 41, 61).

### *Materials*
- Nametags
- Pens
- Refreshments
- Prepared newsprint
- Markers
- Masking tape
- Participant booklet titled "Loved by God, Marked With the Sign of the Cross"

**Symbols of Baptism:**
- Bowl of water, candle, picture of a group of people or the parish directory, baptismal garment, chrism, font
- Booklet insert titled "Rite of Baptism"
- Candle kits

### *Process*
- Welcome
- Climate setting
- Overview
- Opening prayer
- Reflection, symbols
- Discussion and input, "Signs of God's Love"
- Break
- Discussion of godparent qualities
- Godparent information
- Visit church for ritual of Baptism
- Distribute baptismal candle kits
- Reflection of personal faith
- Overview of next session
- Closing prayer and blessing

---

## Session two

### *Welcome*
1) Welcome parents as they arrive.
2) Invite the parents to:
- Fill out a nametag
- Take a "Loved by God, Marked With the Sign of the Cross" booklet to look through
- Get some refreshments

3) Welcome the parents back. Let them know that you are happy to see them again and are looking forward to trying to answer any questions they may have.

### *Climate setting*
Use one of the following icebreakers to help make the transition from their hectic day to a relaxing evening of reflection and learning. The icebreaker will also allow people to become reacquainted.
- Invite each person to complete one of the following sets of phrases:

  Something that I really treasure in my life is ...
  A symbol of that is ...

  Something that I am most looking forward to about Baptism is ...

The thing that makes me uneasy about Baptism is …

Be sure to listen carefully to what each person has to say and allow the group to offer support to one another. If it is appropriate answer any questions or let the group know that you will try to get an answer.

- Invite the group members to respond with the first word that comes to mind when they hear you say a word. Possible words to use would be:  water, light, oil, etc.

Conclude by saying that the same word will have a variety of meanings for different people. Symbols are like that as well. A symbol may hold many meanings for even one person. The symbols of Baptism are one of the aspects of the sacrament that we will be discussing.

### *Overview*

1) Briefly present the objectives for this session. Let the group members know that the symbols and rite of Baptism will affirm the reasons for the theology of Baptism that we discussed the last time you met.

2) Explain that the session will begin with prayer and reflection on faith in their lives.

### *Opening prayer*

1) Invite everyone to look at the cover and page 2 in the booklet. To familiarize the group with the opening prayer:
- Select a leader to read Ephesians 4:4-6.
- Point out the response at the bottom of the booklet cover.
- Invite everyone to pray aloud the "Our Father" at the top of page 2 in the participant booklet.
- Explain to the group members at the conclusion of the prayer they will be asked to share their reflection on the statement from the back cover of the last session's booklet. Read the statement to refresh their memories:

> Someone who has helped me grow in my faith and response to God …
> What they shared with me …

2) Before you begin the prayer invite the parents to sit quietly for a moment, recognizing God's presence and powerful love for each person present.

   3) Pray:

**Leader**: Baptism is a sacrament of faith. Faith is lived out in a community of believers. As the *Catechism of the Catholic Church* reminds us,

"The faith required for Baptism is not a perfect and mature faith, but a beginning that is called to develop. The catechumen or the godparents is asked: 'What do you ask of God's Church?' The response is 'Faith!' " (CCC 1253).

**Reader**: A reading from Ephesians 4:4-6:

There is but "one body and one Spirit, as you were also called to the one hope of your call; one Lord, one baptism, one God and Father of all, who is over all and through all and  in all."

**Response**: We have been called by God and to God we belong.

**Leader**: Together let us pray a prayer that unifies Christians as does Baptism …

**All**: Our Father, who art in heaven, hallowed be thy name. Thy kingdom come. Thy will be done on earth, as it is in heaven. Give us this day our daily bread. And forgive us our trespasses, as we forgive those who trespass against us. And lead us not into temptation, but deliver us from evil. Amen.

### *Shared reflection to the statement:*

> "Someone who has helped me grow in my faith and response to God …"

### *Reflection — Symbols that reveal the richness and meaning of Baptism*

1) As a Baptism team member hangs the sheets of newsprint (prepared prior to the session) around the room, begin the reflection by saying:
- Symbols speak to us in ways which words at times cannot
- Symbols reveal the richness and meaning of Baptism to us

2) Invite the participants to respond to the following statement, "When I see water, it makes me think of _____ …"

3) Record the responses on the posted newsprint labeled "water."

4) Continue the same process for the remaining baptismal symbols: light, white garment, oil.

5) Keep the responses posted by each symbol.

## Symbols

Use the outline below to present the symbols. If possible move from symbol to symbol as you discuss:
   a) The recorded reflections of participants
   b) The meaning of each symbol in the ritual

### Signs of God's love

*Signs of the human world* — Signs and symbols have long played an important role in our lives. We tend to understand and express spiritual realities through the use of physical signs and symbols. Language, gestures, and actions provide a way for people to communicate with each other as social beings. Similarly, we need signs and symbols in our relationship with God (CCC 1146).

*Water* — Water is a basic element in our lives and one of the oldest religious symbols. We cannot live without it. Water changes everything it touches. It is often life-producing, but it can also bring destruction. Water is the primary symbol of Baptism. The powerful transformation that takes place during Baptism occurs as water is poured over the head or there is immersion as a visible sign of participation in the death and resurrection of Christ. With the invocation of the Blessed Trinity, the words, "I baptize you in the name of the Father, and of the Son, and of the Holy Spirit" (CCC 1240), we become one in Christ and then members of the Body of Christ.

*Oil* — Oil is a sign of healing, strength, and of being chosen. During the rite, if the priest or deacon chooses, there may be two anointings. Both are used to symbolize God's presence with us and to give us the healing and strength we will need to live out our commitment to reflect Christ to the world. The baptismal anointing identifies us as the "anointed one," or chosen one, of the Messiah (CCC 1241).

*Light* — The light symbolizes Christ and recalls his words, "I am the light of the world. Whoever follows me will not walk in darkness, but will have the light of life" (John 8:12). During the baptismal rite, the newly-baptized receives a candle lit from the paschal (Easter) candle, which stands beside the altar during the Easter season, and following the Ascension is brought to stand near the baptismal font where it is lit for every Baptism (CCC 1243). At our Baptism we agree to spread the light of Christ wherever we go. At first the parents and godparents accept responsibility for keeping the light burning, but eventually the child must take on the responsibility to keep the faith alive in his/her own heart.

*White garment* — The white garment is a sign of the new life we have in Christ through our Baptism. We remember the words of Saint Paul, "For all of you who were baptized into Christ have clothed yourselves with Christ" (Galatians 3:27) (CCC 1243).

After your presentation of symbols, draw attention to the parish font and offer the following: The font placed in a visible location in the church serves as a constant reminder to all that our life in the Church begins with the sacrament of Baptism. Signifying the tomb in which Christ rose from death to new life, the font is a sign of our mystical sharing in Christ's death and resurrection.

At Baptism we celebrate the child's entrance into the family of God. The community of faith promises to support and guide the child and the family in living out their baptismal promise. Involvement in the community allows their support to be stronger (CCC 1255).

Discussion question: Which symbol speaks the most powerfully to you? Why?

### Break

Invite everyone to:
• Get up and stretch
• Refill their refreshments
• Share some conversation

## Choosing godparents

Choosing the godmother and godfather is a very exciting part of the preparation for Baptism. The title of godparents is not just an honorary title but carries with it many responsibilities to the child, family, and church.

1) Provide the group a few moments of reflection on the qualities that one looks for in godparents, page 3 of the participant booklet.

2) Using the newsprint, record the list as the group brainstorms the qualities to look for in a godparent. Include:
   • Someone whose everyday life reflects his/her faith
   • Someone who is willing to make a long term commitment to you and your child

### Godparents

After everyone has had the opportunity to respond and you have a list of godparent qualities, use the following outline to make a short presentation on godparents.

### Selecting godparents

I. The *Catechism* says this about godparents: "So too is the role of the *godfather* and *godmother*, who must be firm believers, able and ready to help the newly baptized — child or adult — on the road of Christian life. Their task is a truly ecclesial function" (CCC 1255).

II. The godparent is seen as the official representative of the Catholic community, the Mother Church, into which the child is being baptized. The Church asks that the godparents offer their support and help to the parents in the faith formation of the child. The godparents are also called on to be role models of Christian living offering guidance and inspiration to the child (CCC 1255).

III. The responsibility of choosing godparents is a serious one that should be thought about and discussed and prayed about.

The qualifications for the godparent (Canons 872-874) are as follows:

- That he/she be, ordinarily, at least sixteen years of age
- That he/she be Catholic, confirmed, already have received first Eucharist, and lead a life of faith in harmony with the duty he/she is undertaking
- That he/she not be one of the parents of the person being baptized
- That he/she is not under a canonical penalty

IV. Only one sponsor is required for Baptism. The person must fulfill all of the canonical requirements for this role. There can be no more than two sponsors. When pastoral circumstances warrant it, one of these sponsors may be a baptized non-Catholic Christian as a witness of the Baptism.

### Visit the church for the ritual of Baptism

(It is suggested that the priest or deacon who will be baptizing the children present this activity.)

As the group walks through the ritual in the church, the presentation will include:

- The components of the Baptism rite found on the participant insert (page 39)
- The physical movement of the families during the rite: indicate where the parents, godparents, and guests should meet and where they should stand and sit throughout the ritual
- Highlights of the specific roles of parents and godparents during the ritual

## The Rite of Baptism for Children

(Consult with your pastor to adapt this outline to fit the baptismal rite traditions of your parish.)

### I. The reception of the children
**• Greeting**

The presider goes to the entrance of the church (or wherever the parents and godparents are waiting) and welcomes everyone who has come to participate in this very special celebration. The opening words focus on the meaning and importance of Baptism.

**• Questioning**

First the presider will ask three questions of the parents of each child:

"What name do you give this child?"
"What do you ask of God's Church for (name of child)?"

You have asked to have your child baptized. In doing so you are accepting the responsibility of training them in the practice of the faith. It will be your duty to bring them up to keep God's commandments as Christ taught us, by loving God and your neighbor.

"Do you clearly understand what you are undertaking?"

The godparents of each child are then asked:

"Are you ready to help the parents of this child in their duty as Christian parents?"

**• Marked With the Sign of the Cross**

Next the presider claims the child for Christ and welcomes him or her in the name of the Catholic community. He traces the cross on the child's forehead and invites the parents and godparents to do the same (CCC 1235).

**• Celebration of God's Word**

One or more scripture readings may be used. The stories remind us of the implications of our Baptism and of our Christian commitment. The "Rite of Baptism" follows the readings because a sacramental celebration is a response to the Word of God (CCC 1236).

**• Homily**

After the reading the celebrant gives a short homily which will lead those present to a deeper understanding of the mystery of Baptism and the responsibilities of the baptismal commitment.

**• Intercessions**

The Prayer of the Faithful is a prayer of petition for the concerns for the world, for the Church, and for those in need, followed with prayers for the families, the local parish, and the parents.

The presider next invites the community to call upon the saints, which reminds those present that all of the faithful are united in the "communion of saints" and that those who have died can intercede for us.

**• Prayer of exorcism and anointing before Baptism**

The celebrant will offer a short prayer of exorcism meant as a prayer for strengthening. The anointing with the oil on the breast of the child highlights the transformation of the child freed from original sin to a new life in and with Christ (CCC 1237).

### II. Celebration of the sacrament

The celebration turns to the baptismal font. The celebrant briefly reminds the congregation of the meaning of the rite.

**• Blessing and invocation of God over the baptismal waters**

The celebrant blesses the water with a prayer of

thanksgiving, remembering the saving history that water carries.

**• Renunciation of Sin and Profession of Faith**

The adults of the community are called to renew their own Baptism, rejecting sin and professing the faith of the Church. The renunciation of sin and evil, and the profession of the baptismal faith are at the heart of all initiation and discipleship (CCC 1238).

**• Baptism**

After the Profession of Faith, the celebrant asks the parents and godparents one last time if it is their will to baptize the child.

The celebrant then baptizes the child, either by triple immersion or infusion, while saying, "(Name of child), I baptize you in the name of the Father, and of the Son, and of the Holy Spirit" (CCC 1239-1240).

**• Anointing with chrism**

The child's head is anointed with chrism, the same oil used in Confirmation. This anointing is a sign of the child being filled with the Holy Spirit (CCC 1241). This anointing is a link between Baptism and Confirmation, two of the sacraments of initiation.

**• Clothing with white garment**

The celebrant clothes the child with a white garment as a sign of becoming a new creation and being clothed with Christ (CCC 1243).

**• Lighted candle**

The parents are handed candles lit from the Easter candle and are instructed to keep the light of Christ burning brightly for the child so that they may "keep the flame of faith alive in their hearts" (CCC 1243).

**• Conclusion of the rite**

The celebrant stands in front of the altar to address the assembly, to welcome the presence of the newest Christians, and to remind the assembly of the fullness of initiation that will eventually come with Confirmation and Eucharist. Everyone present joins the celebrant in singing or saying the Lord's Prayer. This prayer is offered for the newly baptized and in the spirit of Christian unity.

**• Blessing**

The celebrant first blesses the mothers, then the fathers, then the child, and lastly all others present (CCC 1245). The rite concludes as it began, tracing the Sign of the Cross, this time on oneself.

### Preparing at home

A wonderful way for the families to take part in the baptismal ritual is to prepare the child's Baptism candle.

1) Distribute the Baptism candle instructions and kit.

2) Briefly explain the instructions and materials found in the kit.

### Reflection of personal faith

1) Invite the parents to turn to page 4 of their booklet to the section titled "Faith in my life."

2) Ask the parents to read and think about this section at home prior to the next session:

> What part of the baptismal rite has meaning for me?
> Why?

### Overview of the next session

Give parents a brief idea of topics to be covered at the following meeting:

- Christian parenting
- Parish community
- "Where to go from here"

### Closing prayer and blessing

Invite the parents to bow their heads and receive God's blessing as the following is prayed aloud from the Conclusion of the Rite of Baptism (found on the bottom of page 4 in the participant booklet):

> By God's gift, through water and the Holy Spirit, we are reborn to everlasting life. In God's goodness, may he continue to pour out blessings upon all present, who are God's sons and daughters. May God make them always, wherever they may be, faithful members of his holy people. May God send peace upon all who are gathered here, in Christ Jesus our Lord.
>
> **All**: Amen (paraphrased from the "Rite of Baptism").

### Final notes

1) Remind the group of the dates and times of future classes.

2) Invite the parents to stay after if they have any questions or concerns that they would like to discuss with a member of the team.

# *The Making of a Christian Home*

## Session three overview

### Objectives

- To provide parents with the opportunity to discuss and affirm their vocation as Christian parents.
- To give parents helpful information about faith development and Catholic formation of their child.
- To help parents understand that their parish community not only welcomes their participation but has a great deal to offer them.

### Preparation

- Copy back to back and fold participant booklet "The Making of a Christian Home" (see page 43).
- Obtain copies of parish's handbook OR prepare parish insert (see page 62).
- Copy and cut apart the Christian Family Life (CFL) cards (see page 45).
- Read through CFL notes (see page 22).
- Invite someone from the parish to come to the session and talk about the various parish organizations and ministries.

### Materials

- Nametags
- Markers
- Pens
- Christian Family Life (CFL) cards
- Newsprint
- Masking tape
- Participant booklet titled "The Making of a Christian Home"
- Refreshments

### Process

- Welcome
- Climate setting
- Overview
- Opening prayer
- Christian Family Life cards activity
- Break
- Reflection, "Families of Faith"
- Discussion and input, "Rely on Your Catholic Community"
- Reflection of personal faith
- Closing prayer and blessing

---

## Session three

### Welcome

1) Welcome parents as they arrive.

2) Invite the parents to:

- Fill out a nametag
- Take a "Recognizing God's Presence in Our Family" booklet to look through
- Complete the statement at the top of page 3
- Get some refreshments

3) Thank the families for coming together again. Their attendance is a sign that they understand the importance of the responsibility they are assuming as Christian parents.

### Climate setting

Invite each person to briefly introduce him- or herself for any new members of the group and then to do one of the following:

- Ask participants to share their thoughts on the phrase from participant booklet 2 "Reflection of personal faith." To refresh their memories reread the phrase for the group:

> The part of the rite that has the most meaning for me is …
> Why?

Conclude by reminding the group that both the rite and symbols speak to us in a powerful way about God's presence and movement in our lives.

- Complete the phrases:

> The best part of being a parent is …
> Something that makes me uneasy about being a parent is …

Conclude by saying, while there are many blessings that come with being a parent, there are also some challenges and concerns. Choosing to raise their child in a Christian home along with the support of their family and Catholic community will make the difference in their family life.

### Overview

Remind the parents that allowing their child to receive Baptism is a sign of their love for their child. The child is baptized into Christ. Together the parents and the Catholic community make a strong statement of faith. The community and parents promise to nourish the child in a loving home and community. As the light and love of Christ shines through them, the children will begin to accept God's

love on their own. Discovering how we are called to live the Gospel so our children can experience it becomes the challenge.

1) Explain that at this session the members will have the opportunity to explore and discuss this challenge.

2) Briefly present the objectives for this session.

### *Opening prayer*

1) Invite everyone to look at the cover and page 1 of the parent booklet. Familiarize the group with the opening prayer by doing the following:

- Select a leader to read Ephesians 3:14-19.
- Point out the response at the bottom of the booklet cover.
- Invite everyone to pray aloud the "Prayer of Saint Francis" found at the bottom of page 2 in their booklet (note: the group may be divided in half, with each group taking one line at a time of the first two stanzas and doing the last stanza together).
- Explain to group members at the conclusion of the prayer that they will be asked to share their reflections to the statement on page 2 of their booklet.

2) Before you begin the prayer, invite the parents to sit quietly for a moment, recognizing the presence of God and the importance of God in the life of their families.

3) Pray:

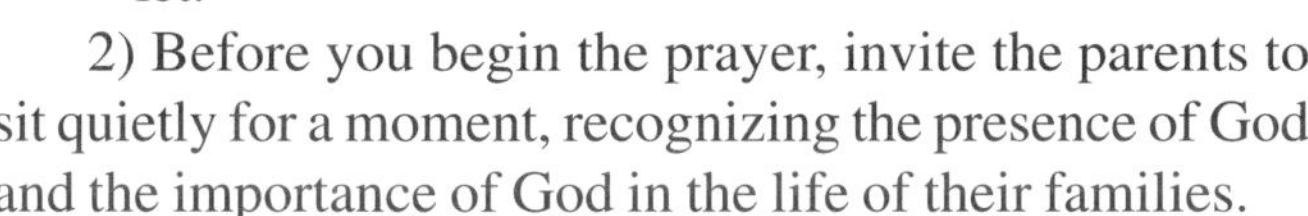

**Leader**: A reading from Ephesians 3:14-19:

"For this reason I kneel before the Father, from whom every family in heaven and on earth is named, that he may grant you in accord with the riches of his glory to be strengthened with power through his Spirit in the inner self, and that Christ may dwell in your hearts through faith; that you, rooted and grounded in love, may have strength to comprehend with all the holy ones what is the breadth and length and height and depth, and to know the love of Christ that surpasses knowledge, so that you may be filled with all the fullness of God."

**Response**: Open our hearts, O God.

**Leader**: There is a prayer ascribed to Saint Francis of Assisi which is reflective of our daily vocation as parents.

**All**: Lord, make me an instrument of your peace.
Where there is hatred, let me sow love;
Where there is injury, pardon;
Where there is doubt, faith;
Where there is despair, hope;
Where there is darkness, light;
And where there is sadness, joy.
O Divine Master, grant that I may not so
   much seek to be consoled as to console,
To be understood as to understand,
To be loved as to love;

For it is in giving that we receive,
It is in pardoning that we are pardoned,
And it is in dying that we are born to
   eternal life.
           Amen.

### *Shared reflection to the statement:*

"How can I be an image of the light of Christ to the world? At home? At work?"

### *Christian Family Life activity*

1) Read the following quote from the *Catechism of the Catholic Church* as the group looks at it on page 3 of the booklet for this session: "*Education in the faith by the parents should begin in the child's earliest years. This already happens when the family members help one another to grow in faith by the witness of a Christian life in keeping with the Gospel. Family catechesis precedes, accompanies, and enriches other forms of instruction in the faith. Parents have the mission of teaching their children to pray and to discover their vocation as children of God. The parish is the Eucharistic community and the heart of the liturgical life of Christian families; it is a privileged place for the catechesis of children and parents*" (CCC 2226).

2) Ask the question, "Where do we begin?" Draw into focus the religious experience of a young child by offering the following:

The religious formation of a child begins before birth. It is really the formation of the whole person in body, mind, and spirit. The physical care and love that we give a child are an important part of their religious formation. Everything that we do for and with the child helps to form the child in the image and likeness of God. It is through your love and patience that your child will first learn the love and patience of God. It is through your forgiveness and reconciling that your child will first learn about God's gift of forgiveness and healing. It is by praying with you that your child will learn to pray.

3) Put the Christian Family Life (CFL) cards in a stack, while explaining that each card states actions found to be characteristic of Christian families.

4) Hand the stack to a person in the group and ask that he/she take the top card from the pile. Ask the person to comment on:

- How the stated action might be beneficial to the family
- How easy or difficult it would be to do

After the member responds to the statements, others in the group may add additional comments.

The member drawing the card has the option of commenting on the card, passing that card to the next person, or passing the cards altogether.

5) The activity continues with everyone listening carefully to the comments offered. Remind the group that there are no right or wrong responses due to the uniqueness of each family.

### *CFL notes and cards*

(*Note: The participants should be encouraged to give most of the input for the CFL cards, however the information below is provided if added comments are needed.*)

**Card 1 — Parents modeling a Christian lifestyle**

When you get up to feed your hungry infant in the middle of the night, comfort and care for your child when he or she is sick, or offer a hug when he or she falls, you are a reflection of a loving and understanding God. It is also good to remember that children are exceptional imitators. Much to our delight and at times dismay, they repeat a great deal of what they see, hear, and experience.

**Card 2 — Praying together**

No matter what our age is, we learn to pray by praying. Your child will learn to pray by praying with you. The words come from our hearts and flow from our lives. These prayers can be spontaneous, short family blessings, or more traditional in nature. Prayer in your home must be suited to your family. What is important is that prayer becomes a basic part of your lives as you grow in faith together.

**Card 3 — Sharing stories**

We all remember stories that have been shared with us. Some of our very best times together as families are the times we spend sharing stories. The stories of our own lives and experiences, stories about our ancestors, stories about our faith, and stories from scripture. These stories draw us together and share our Christian values, morals, and our lives in a way that nothing else could.

**Card 4 — Treating one another with love and respect**

We have been commanded to love one another as God loves us. Our self-image and feelings of self-worth are often a reflection of the approval, recognition, and love of our families. Respect is another important part of loving relationships. Respect means to hold someone in high regard or esteem. Every member of a family from the oldest to the youngest should feel that he or she is respected.

**Card 5 — Forgiving and reconciling**

Families live in close contact with each other and their rough edges are exposed. Learning to forgive each other and to reconcile our differences strengthens the bond of love in families and makes the love and forgiveness of God more real in our lives. Children will learn to forgive when they see forgiveness as part of everyday life.

**Card 6 — Sharing meals together**

It may be difficult at times but it is important to gather regularly to eat together. As the food is shared so are the events of their lives. This time spent together builds a sense of belonging and commitment. The meal also provides the family with an opportunity for family prayer and gives the members a sense of gratitude for what has been given to them.

6) Conclude by saying that we have a great deal to look forward to as parents as we grow in faith with our children.

### *Break*

Invite everyone to:
- Get up and stretch
- Refill their refreshments
- Share some conversation

### *Reflection — families of faith*

This activity offers the group members the opportunity to think about and discuss Christian parenting with other parents.

1) Ask group members to open the participant booklet to page 3.

2) Allow parents a few minutes to read through and to fill out this page. Invite them to choose one or two of the questions that they feel comfortable talking about with the group. As this task is explained emphasize once again that there are no specifically right or wrong answers.

How will Christian parenting show in the way you raise your child?

What ritual (tradition) in your family of origin meant the most to you as a child?

Who was the most loving person in your life when you were a child? Is it important to say "I love you"? Why?

How do you want your child to see God?

What will you do to nurture the faith of your family?

3) After each parent has had the opportunity to comment on two of the questions, summarize what has been said. Remind the parents that they are never alone in the task of raising their child. God has given us the gift of the Holy Spirit to be with us and guide us.

### *Rely on your Catholic community*

Remind the parents that their Catholic community has a great deal to offer their families. Provide the following input:

**The Mass**

Attend Mass each Sunday and as often as you are able as a family. It is an opportunity to celebrate the Eucharist with other Catholics, rejuvenate yourself, and strengthen your family.

**The sacraments**

Celebrate the sacraments of the Church. The sacraments are meant to strengthen our relationship with Christ, fill us with grace, and empower us to be His disciples.

**The faith formation of children**

The Church will help you with your child's Catholic formation by offering religious education through the early childhood religious formation program, Catholic day school, or evening or after-school religious education program.

**The continued faith formation of the parents**

Don't forget about your own faith journey. The commitment that we make at Baptism is a lifelong one. The most important thing you can do for your family is to make time for yourself and your spouse to grow in God's spirit both in heart and mind.

1) Invite the parish representative to familiarize the participants with the parish groups and activities. It may be surprising to discover which parish ministries interest individuals in the group.

2) Extend an invitation to the parents to further investigate the ministries and organizations which interest them. Use the parish handbook or the insert to point out the meeting dates, times, places, and contact people for each of these parish groups.

Explain that if the time for their participation in parish life is not possible now with a new baby, the invitation to become involved with a parish group will always be there.

### *Reflection of personal faith*

1) Invite the parents to turn to page 4 of their booklet to the section titled "Faith in my life."

2) Ask the parents to explore the following question as they reflect upon what they learned during these Baptism preparation sessions:

How will I continue to grow in my faith?

### *Closing prayer and blessing*

Invite the parents to bow their heads and receive God's blessing as the following is read aloud from page 4 of the booklet:

God is the giver of life.
May God bless the parents of this child.
They will be the first teachers of their child in the way of faith.
May they also be the best teachers, bearing witness to the faith by what they do and say.
**All**: Amen (paraphrased from the "Rite of Baptism").

### *Final notes*

Thank the parents for their participation. Express the Church's excitement about the upcoming celebration of Baptism. Invite the parents to stay after class if they have any questions that they would like to ask one of the team members.

*For your notes ...*

Dear

As the coordinator of the Baptism preparation team, I am always anxious to find new people to join our ministry. The team is made up of people from the parish who gather to welcome and assist in the preparation of parents having their children baptized. You would be a great addition to our team!

We are looking for people, such as yourself, who are faith-filled Catholics and willing to be welcoming members of our community. As part of the team, you would be taking an active role in our church community. It is amazing how our faith deepens as it is shared with others.

Please consider your involvement in this ministry. I would be happy to discuss this ministry with you further if you are interested.

God bless you!

*"Christ, from whom the whole body, joined and held together by every supporting ligament, with the proper functioning of each part, brings about the body's growth and builds itself up in love" (Ephesians 4:16).*

Personalize the volunteer interest letter by supplying the following:

- Parish letterhead
- The date
- The person to whom the letter is being sent
- Name and signature of team coordinator
- Phone number at which coordinator may be reached

# *Session planning sheet*

**session #______**

*Objectives:*

*Preparation:*

*Materials:*

*Welcome*                    **session #______**                    **page #______**

*Climate setting*                **session #______**                    **page #______**

*Participant session overview:*

*Opening prayer*                **session #______**                    **page #______**

*Topic*                              session # _______                          page #______

*Topic 2*                            session # _______                          page # ______

*Break*

*Topic 3*                            session # _______                          page # ______

*Reflection of personal faith:*  session # _______                    page # ______

*Overview of next session:*

*Closing blessing*                   session # ______                           page # _______

*Additional notes:*

Dear

Your child's Baptism will be a time for great joy and celebration for you, your family, and your Catholic community. We are anxious to help you prepare for this very special event. During the sessions we will discuss the meaning and importance of the Rite of Baptism, the symbols, and our vocation as Christian parents.

We will be meeting:

We look forward to meeting you and sharing this faith-filled time.

Sincerely,


Tis
a blessing
to be

Dear

Your child's Baptism will be a time for great joy and celebration for you, your family, and your Catholic community. We are anxious to help you prepare for this very special event. During the sessions we will discuss the meaning and importance of the Rite of Baptism, the symbols, and our vocation as Christian parents.

We will be meeting:

We look forward to meeting you and sharing this faith-filled time.

Sincerely,

Personalize this note of welcome by supplying the following information:
- Parish letterhead
- The date
- The names of the parents receiving the letter
- Number of sessions
- Meeting dates
- Meeting time (beginning-end)
- Meeting place
- Availability of child care
- Signed by team members/session leaders

## Faith in my life

Someone who has helped me grow in my faith and response to God:

_______________________________

_______________________________

What they shared with me:

_______________________________

_______________________________

### Blessing

God, through his Son, the Virgin Mary's Child, has brought joy to all Christian parents, as they see the hope of eternal life shine on their children. May God bless the parents of these children. May they be one with them in thanking God forever in heaven, in Christ Jesus our Lord.

Amen

*(paraphrased from the "Rite of Baptism").*

## Promised and Made New
*in*
# BAPTISM

"Truly you have formed my inmost
  being;
  you knit me in my mother's womb.
I give you thanks that I am fearfully,
  wonderfully made;
  wonderful are your works.
My soul also you knew full well;
  nor was my frame unknown to you
When I was made in secret,
  when I was fashioned in the depths
  of the earth"  (Psalm 139:13-15).

*Thankful are we, loving God,
for this precious gift of life.*

## When I heard you were coming, I felt:

_______________________________________

_______________________________________

_______________________________________

_______________________________________

_______________________________________

We are filled with awe and wonder,
as we give you thanks and praise,
loving God. These new lives from
your hands are treasures to be cherished always. As we gather here
open our hearts and minds, remembering that it is through water and
the word that we receive your light
and life. Amen.

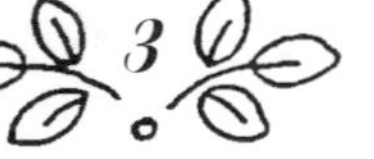

## What meaning does Baptism have for you?

Rate each phrase with a number that best describes your understanding of Baptism.

_______________________________________

| 1 | 2 | 3 | 4 | 5 |
|---|---|---|---|---|
| Very close | | | | Very different |

_____ An opportunity for the Catholic community to welcome and pledge support to the child and parents.

_____ A rite to free the child from original sin.

_____ A commitment to help the child know and follow Jesus and learn about the faith.

_____ A day when your child is initiated into the life of Christ, thus becoming a "new creation."

_____ A time for parents to nourish their own faith life so that they can support the gift of faith they share with their child.

# You Are Chosen ...

*"There is a season for everything, a time for every purpose under heaven"* (NRSV) Ecclesiastes 3:1.

**Your child is a miracle, a gift from God's hands**, given to you at just the right time to touch your lives and fill your hearts with love and joy. From the love you have for each other, God has called forth this beautiful creation. God has a deep and eternal love for you and your child. With God's help, you will nurture, care for, and love this child. As you watch your child grow and experience new things in life, your faith in God and yourself will be affirmed. What a privilege it is to become a parent.

**Your Catholic community is delighted** that you have chosen to have your child baptized. At Baptism we receive and celebrate God's free gift of grace and salvation through Christ. It is really God who has chosen us. Thus Baptism is the beginning of a lifelong journey in knowing and following Jesus. Baptism is also the first sacrament of initiation; later will come Confirmation and first Eucharist. The Catholic community welcomes your child with open arms and extends its loving support in living a life that reflects Jesus to the world.

**You are called to grow in God's love with your child**. As you share your faith with your child, your relationship with God will deepen. As you pray with your family, attend Mass and share your Christian values, your family will grow closer together in love for one another and God. Your child's Baptism is only the beginning!

*Commonly asked questions ...*
**What is original sin?**
Original sin is a condition of separation from God and of our personal weakness in living as people of God. Original sin is removed when we are filled with the love and grace of Christ through the gift of Baptism.

**What happens to a baby who dies without Baptism?**
Scripture and tradition reveal a God who loves us from our very conception. The love of God is mysterious and powerful, all-encompassing, and directed to eternal life. This love is so great that He sent Jesus to teach us how to live and to receive eternal life. Jesus' tenderness toward children was expressed when he said, "Let the children come to me, do not hinder them," which gives us hope that all children will be given eternal happiness.

*Your questions ...*

_______________________________

_______________________________

_______________________________

_______________________________

_______________________________

_______________________________

_______________________________

Insert for session 1
 • Copy "You Are Chosen …" (back to back, on half-sheets of paper).

1 What did the Baptisms performed by John the Baptist on the Jordan River symbolize?

6 How did the rise of Christianity during the Roman Empire change the initiation rite?

2 Why did the apostles baptize? When did they begin to baptize?

7 Why did Baptisms move away from the traditional Easter Vigil ceremony?

3 What was the norm for Baptisms in the early Christian Church?

8 How did Baptism and Confirmation become separated from one another?

4 What steps did the early Christians take to become members of the Church?

9 What happened as infant Baptisms became the norm?

5 What was the role of the sponsor in the early Church's process of initiation?

10 What changes took place at Vatican II that affected the way Baptisms are celebrated today?

**6** As the state and Church grew much closer together, so did citizenship and initiation. Preparation requirements for initiation eased as Christianity was practiced openly.

**7** Due to the high infant mortality rate of this period, parents felt it might be too risky to wait until the Easter Vigil to have the infants baptized. These concerns were heightened by the teachings of Saint Augustine tied to the scriptures in Genesis.

**8** The bishops were not able to keep up with all of the requested initiations in their widely-stretched dioceses. So the Baptisms and Eucharists were assigned to the local priest, and the anointing with chrism or Confirmation continued to be the responsibility of the bishops.

**9** Since the candidate could not speak, the godparents and parents recited the prayers and answered for the infant. The ceremony became a private event taking place in the home with only those of the community wishing to attend to be present.

**10** Vatican II Council returned the Church to the initiation model similar to the early Church, one of conversion and formation. For infants, initiation would now only begin with Baptism. The formation of the child would continue with the aid of the parents, godparents, and the Church community. The sacraments of Baptism, Confirmation, and Eucharist form today's initiation (CCC 1212).

**1** These Baptisms symbolized a repentance of sin (Matthew 3:11). Jesus and his disciples were among those who were baptized with water by John the Baptist on the Jordan.

**2** The apostles were called to baptize when Jesus appeared to them at Galilee. He told the eleven apostles to go and "Baptize in the name of the Father, and of the son, and of the Holy Spirit" (Matthew 28:18-20). On Pentecost the apostles baptized three thousand (Acts 2:38-41).

**3** In the early Church adults were the norm for Christian Baptisms. Although infants were not specifically mentioned as being baptized (CCC 1252) the early Church must have recognized the domestic church that dwelled within the family because it was customary to convert entire households.

**4** Membership included these steps: 1) period of instruction on Church teachings referred to as a catechumenate period, lasting about three years; 2) Baptism at Easter Vigil — submerging in water to signify the dying and rising with Christ; 3) seal — anointed with chrism by the bishop; 4) joining in the celebration of Eucharist with the full community, dressed in a white garment to symbolize the enveloping of Christ (Galatians 3:27).

**5** The sponsor was a member of the Church community who would vouch for the candidate's intentions and would assist in their preparation. Today, this role is similar to that of the "godparent" who is to assist the parents in guiding the infant on his/her spiritual journey (CCC 1255).

## Faith in my life

What part of the baptismal rite has meaning for me?

_______________________________________________

Why? __________________________________________

_______________________________________________

_______________________________________________

_______________________________________________

_______________________________________________

*Blessing*

By God's gift, through water and the Holy Spirit, we are reborn to everlasting life. In God's goodness, may he continue to pour out blessings upon all present, who are God's sons and daughters. May God make them always, wherever they may be, faithful members of his holy people. May God send peace to all who are gathered here, in Christ Jesus our Lord.

Amen

*(paraphrased from the "Rite of Baptism").*

# Loved by God,

## Marked With the Sign of the Cross

There is but "one body and one Spirit, as you were also called to the one hope of your call; one Lord, one faith, one baptism; one God and Father of all, who is over all and through all and in all"

(Ephesians 4:4-6).

**We have been called by God and to God we belong.**

Our Father, who art in heaven, hallowed be thy name. Thy kingdom come. Thy will be done on earth, as it is in heaven. Give us this day our  daily bread. And forgive us our trespasses, as we forgive those who trespass against us. And lead us not into temptation, but deliver us from evil. Amen.

## Symbols and Scripture

### water

"I will sprinkle clean water upon you to cleanse you from all your impurities … I will give you a new heart and place a new spirit within you" (Ezekiel 36:25-26).

### light

"Jesus spoke to them again, saying, 'I am the light of the world. Whoever follows me will not walk in darkness' " (John 8:12).

### oil

"You are a 'chosen race, a royal priesthood, a holy nation, a people of his own, so that you may announce the praises of him' " (1 Peter 2:9).

### white garment

"For all of you who were baptized into Christ have clothed yourselves with Christ" (Galatians 3:26-28).

The symbol which speaks most powerfully to me:

_______________________________

_______________________________

_______________________________

_______________________________

## Godparents

The qualities I value in a godparent are:

_______________________________

_______________________________

People I have thought about as possible godparents are:

_______________________________

_______________________________

Why?

_______________________________

_______________________________

_______________________________

# Rite of Baptism

## I. The Reception of the Children

- **Greeting**

  The celebrant goes to the entrance of the church and welcomes everyone to this very special celebration.

- **Questioning**

  The celebrant will ask three questions of the parents:

  "What name do you give this child?"

  "What do you ask of God's Church for (name of child)?"

  "Do you clearly understand what you are undertaking?"

  The godparents of each child will be asked,

  "Are you ready to help the parents of this child in their duty as Christian parents?"

- **Marked With the Sign of the Cross**

  The celebrant traces the cross on the child's forehead and invites the parents and godparents to do the same.

- **Celebration of God's Word**

  One or more scripture readings may be used.

- **Homily**

  The celebrant gives a short homily to lead those present to a deeper understanding of the mystery of Baptism and the responsibilities of the baptismal commitment.

- **Intercessions**

  The Prayer of the Faithful is a prayer of petition for the concerns for the world.

- **Prayer of Exorcism and Anointing before Baptism**

  The celebrant will offer a short prayer of exorcism and anoint the child's breast with the oil as a sign of strengthening.

## II. Celebration of the Sacrament

The celebration moves to the baptismal font.

- **Blessing and Invocation of God over the Baptismal Waters**

  The celebrant blesses the water with a prayer of thanksgiving.

- **Baptism**

  After the Profession of Faith, the celebrant asks the parents and godparents one last time if it is their will to baptize the child.

  The celebrant then baptizes the child either by immersion or infusion.

- **Anointing With Chrism**

  The child's head is anointed with chrism as a sign of the child being filled with the Holy Spirit.

- **Clothing With White Garment**

  The celebrant clothes the child with a white garment as a sign of becoming a new creation and being clothed with Christ.

- **Lighted Candle**

  The parents are handed candles lit from the paschal candle.

- **Conclusion of the Rite**

  The celebrant welcomes the newly baptized child. Everyone present joins the celebrant in singing or saying the Lord's Prayer.

- **Blessing**

  The celebrant first blesses the mothers, the fathers, the child, and lastly all others present. The rite concludes as it began, tracing the Sign of the Cross, this time on oneself.

Insert for session 2
Copy "Rite of Baptism" (back-to-back, on half-sheets of paper).

# *Ideas for decorating a Baptism candle*

**Helpful steps:**
1) Invite a godparent or other special person to be involved with this activity.
2) Design your child's candle using the suggested ideas and patterns, or create your own.
3) Write your child's name and the date of the Baptism on the candle.
4) When selecting colors use red, blue, gold, silver.

### *Fabric paint candle*

**Materials**: squeeze bottle, fabric paint, white candle
1) Decide on a design.
2) Squeeze tiny drops of fabric paint onto the candle to create the design.
3) Let dry completely.

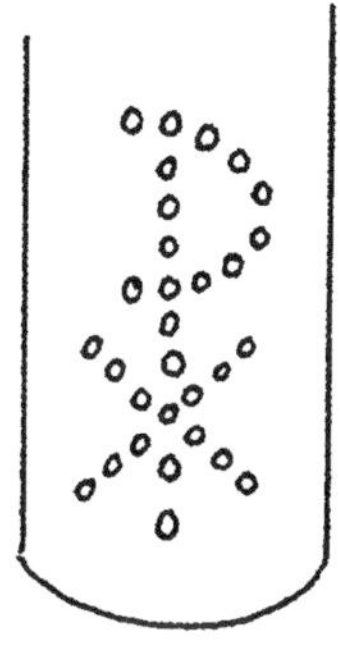

### *Contact paper candle*

**Materials**: solid colored or metallic contact paper, pencil, scissors, white candle
1) Draw the pattern of the symbol or design on the backing side of the contact paper.
2) Using scissors cut out the design.
3) Peel away the backing of the contact paper and place the tacky side of the symbol on the candle.

### *Acrylic painted candle*

**Materials**: acrylic paints, paint brush, white candle
1) Select a design.
2) Paint design on the candle using acrylic paints.

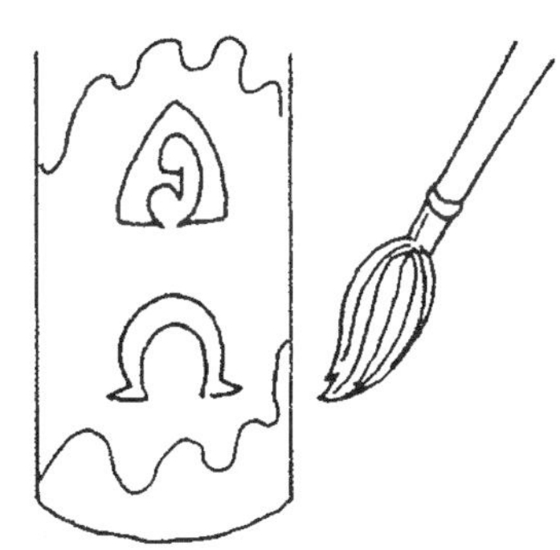

*Permanent marker candle*
**Materials**: white candle, permanent markers
1) Choose a design.
2) Use markers to draw design onto the candle.
3) Let dry completely.

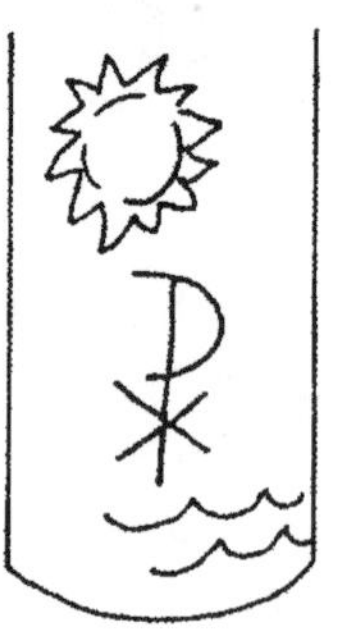

*Heat point of pin in the flame of the warming candle*

*Beaded candle*
**Materials**: glass seed beads, warming candle, straight pin, white candle
1) Use the straight pin to pick up a glass bead. Slide the bead up the pin away from the pin point.
2) Heat the point of the pin on the flame of the warming candle.
3) Touch the hot pin point to the exact place on the baptismal candle that you would like the bead to remain. (The hot pin melts the wax on the baptismal candle just enough to hold the bead in place.)
5) Slide the bead off the pin.
6) Continue adding beads in this manner until the design is complete.

*Candle with ribbons*
**Materials**: narrow satin ribbon, white candle, (optional: charms)
   Tie ribbons around the bottom of the candle leaving long streamers hanging.

Who was the most loving person in my life as a child?

Is it important to say "I love you"?

Why?

How do I want my child to see God?

What will I do to nurture the faith of my family?

## Faith in my life

How will I continue to grow in my faith?

## Blessing

God is the giver of life. May God bless the parents of this child. They will be the first teachers of their child in the way of faith. May they also be the best teachers, bearing witness to the faith by what they do and say.

Amen

*(paraphrased from the "Rite of Baptism").*

# The Making of a Christian Home

"For this reason I kneel before the Father, from whom every family in heaven and on earth is named, that he may grant you in accord with the riches of his glory to be strengthened with power through his Spirit in the inner self, and that Christ may dwell in your hearts through faith; that you, rooted and grounded in love, may have strength to comprehend with all the holy ones what is the breadth and length and height and depth, and to know the love of Christ that surpasses knowledge, so that you may be filled with all the fullness of God"
(Ephesians 3:14-19).

*Open our hearts, O God.*

How can I be an image of the light of Christ to the world? _______

At home: _______

At work: _______

## Prayer of Saint Francis

Lord, make me an instrument of your peace.
Where there is hatred, let me sow love;
Where there is injury, pardon;
Where there is doubt, faith;
Where there is despair, hope;
Where there is darkness, light;
And where there is sadness, joy.

O Divine Master, grant that I may not so much
    seek to be consoled as to console,
To be understood as to understand,
To be loved as to love;

For it is in giving that we receive,
It is in pardoning that we are pardoned,
And it is in dying that we are born to eternal
    life.

                                        Amen.

"*Education in the faith* by the parents should begin in the child's earliest years. This already happens when family members help one another to grow in faith by the witness of a Christian life in keeping with the Gospel. Family catechesis precedes, accompanies, and enriches other forms of instruction in the faith. Parents have the mission of teaching their children to pray and to discover their vocation as children of God. The parish is the Eucharistic community and the heart of the liturgical life of Christian families; it is a privileged place for the catechesis of children and parents" (CCC 2226).

## Christian parenting

How will Christian parenting show in the way I raise my child?
_______
_______
_______
_______

What tradition in my family meant the most to me as a child?
_______
_______
_______
_______

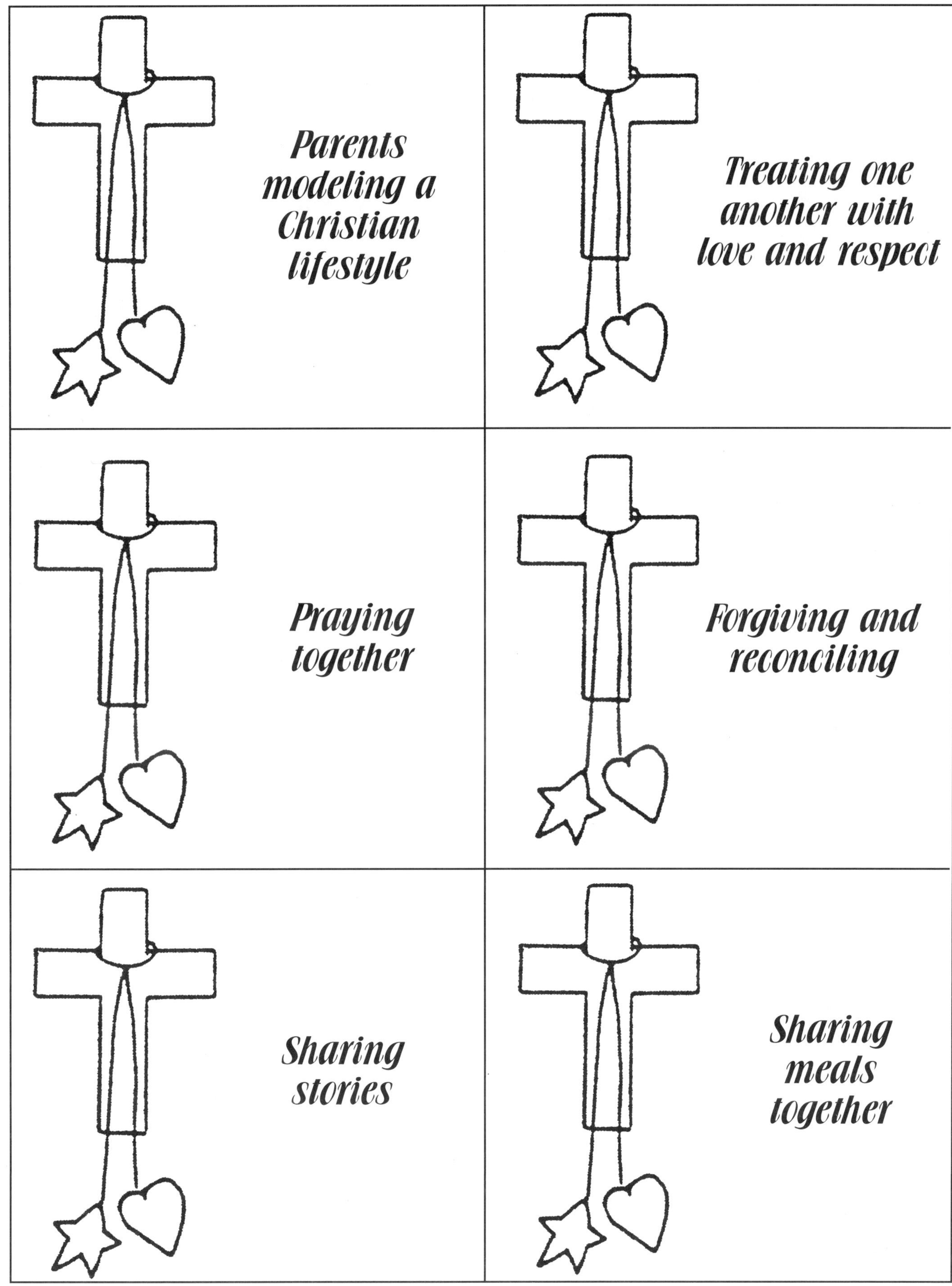
Parents modeling a Christian lifestyle
Treating one another with love and respect
Praying together
Forgiving and reconciling
Sharing stories
Sharing meals together

CFL Cards — cut at lines

# Clip Art

Copy and cut apart clip art as needed.

# *BAPTISM INFORMATION*

**Child's name** _______________________________________________________
            (First)            (Middle)              (Last)

**Birth** ___________________________________________________________
            (Date)              (City, State)

**Father** _________________________________________ **Religion** __________
        (First)    (Middle)    (Last)

**Mother** _________________________________________ **Religion** __________
        (First)   (Middle/Maiden)   (Last)

**Address** _______________________________________ **Phone #** __________
        (Street)                                        (Home)

_______________________________________ __________
        (State, Zip Code)                               (Work)

**Godparent** _____________________________________ **Religion** __________

**Godparent** _____________________________________ **Religion** __________

**Baptism date requested** _________________________ **Time** __________

**Priest /Deacon celebrating** ___________________________________________

**Notes:**

Baptism Information
• Adapt use of this form for your parish
• Use to obtain information needed for baptismal certificate
• Distribute after session that explores the topic of "Godparents"
    Mail in a parish envelope
    Hand-deliver during session

# Baptism preparation team follow-up

*Adapt this sample follow-up form to help the team evaluate each session.*
- *Give team members this form right at the conclusion of the session. (An alternative would be to meet with the team for a few minutes, asking the following questions.)*
- *Ask them to take a minute to fill it out and return it before they leave.*

## Sample of follow-up form

*Thank you for being an important part of this ministry.*
*Please take a few minutes to fill out this follow-up form.*
*Your input is important to us!*

In general, how do you feel this session went?

Did you have the needed resources and enough participant materials?

Is there anything else that would have been helpful to have?

Were there any questions that you felt uncomfortable answering?

Is there anyone in the group whom you would like a parish staff member to contact with a phone call or visit?
Name:
Purpose:

Do you have any suggestions to improve this session the next time?

# Program evaluation participant follow-up

*For best results …*
- *Hand out a short, simple evaluation form during the break of the last session.*
- *Invite participants to take a few minutes to fill it out before the end of the session when you will collect the forms.*
- *Collect the forms at the end of the session and thank the participants for their input.*

## Sample evaluation form

*Please take a few minutes to answer the questions below. Your comments and suggestions will help us improve the sessions. Thank you!*

How would you evaluate the sessions?

Session one

_____ Excellent          _____Very good          _____Fair          _____Poor

Session two

_____ Excellent          _____Very good          _____Fair          _____Poor

Session three

_____ Excellent          _____Very good          _____Fair          _____Poor

What part of the program was the most helpful?

What was the most valuable or interesting discovery you made?

Do you have any comments or suggestions to help improve the sessions?

*Feel free to discuss your comments with one of the team members.*

# *White garments*
## *pattern and directions*

## Materials

3/4 yard of 45-inch wide piece of white fabric, 5 yards of gold ribbon, thread, chalk or carbon to trace design, scissors

*(Note: This much material will make four garments.)*

## Instructions

1) Open fabric layout as diagramed; fabric should be folded in half with fold at top.

2) Pin enlarged pattern pieces to fabric, lining up dotted line with the fold of the fabric as indicated.

3) Cut out garment.

4) Cut three-inch slit down from center back neckline.

5) Trace the design on the front of garment piece as marked on pattern.

6) Hand or machine sew the gold ribbon to the front of the garment, using the traced design as a guide.

7) Turn under, press, and sew a 1/4 inch hem around all of the raw edges of the garment. **Do not** sew the sides together. The garment is simply slipped over the baby's head and rests on the shoulders.

8) Trim raw edges of neckline opening with gold ribbon.

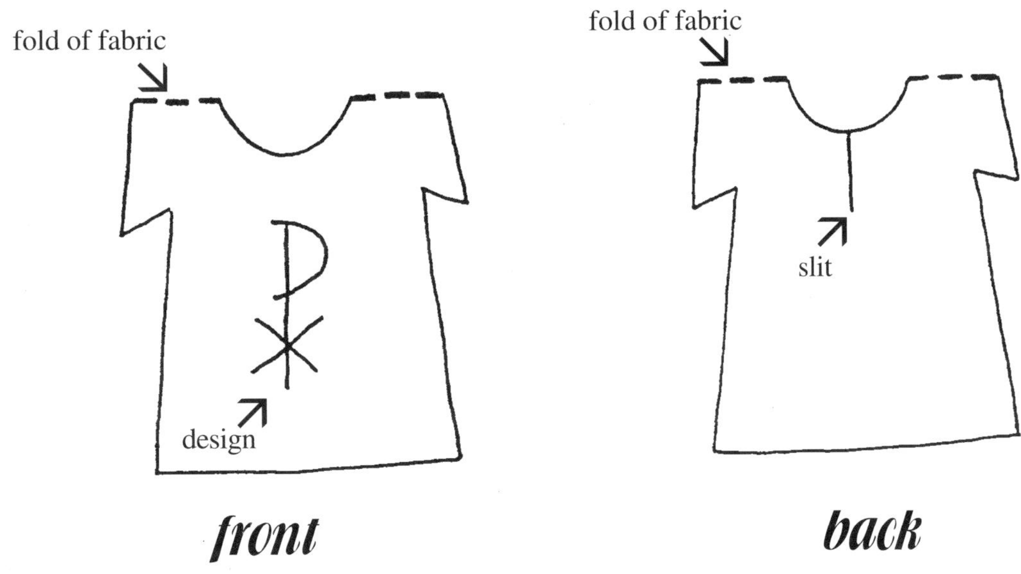

Enlarge the pattern below on a copier by 170% OR enlarge to an 11x14 sheet of paper.

**Hem raw edges. Do not sew side seams together.**
**Garment is slipped over the baby's shoulders.**



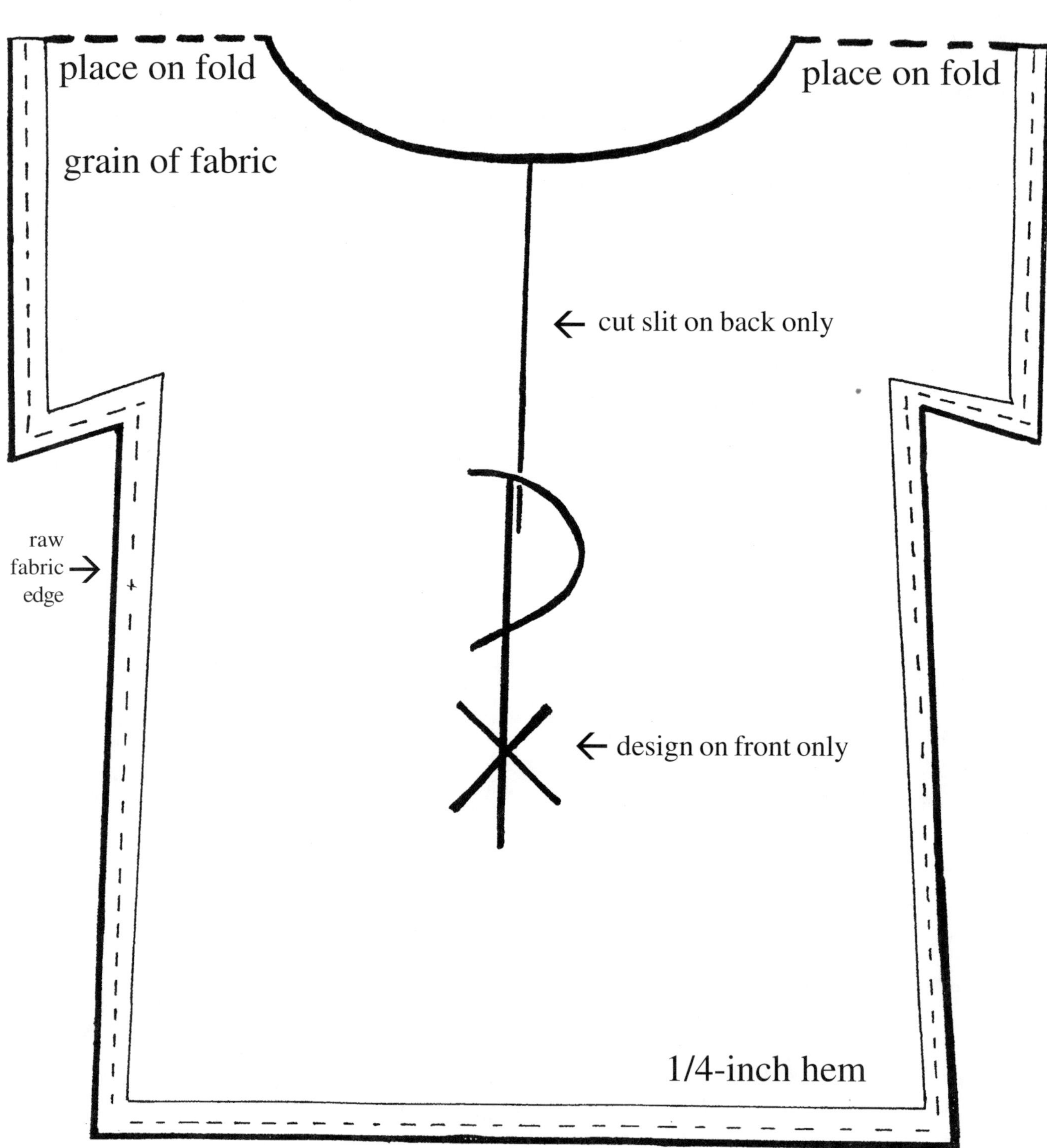

Be helpful in your godchild's preparation and reception of the other sacraments. First Communion and Confirmation are the sacraments which will complete your godchild's initiation into the Catholic community. Support the parents in providing formal religious formation for your godchild. Ask your godchild about his/her formation from time to time.

Most importantly, keep your godchild in your daily prayers and be a constant reflection of God's unconditional love for him/her.

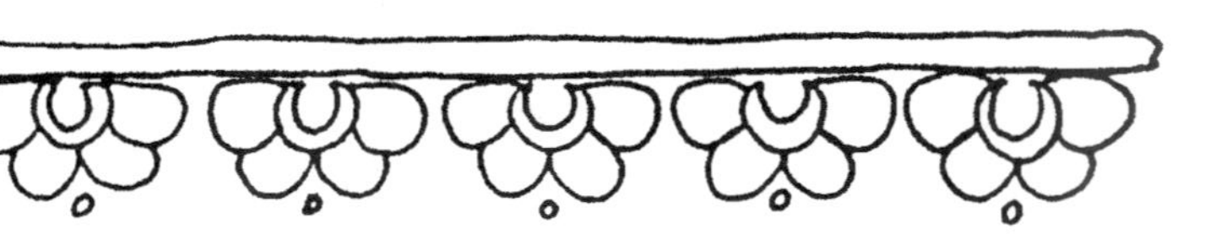

"See what love the
Father has bestowed on us,
that we may be called
the children of God.
Yet so we are"
(1 John 3:1).

*God bless you and your godchild!*

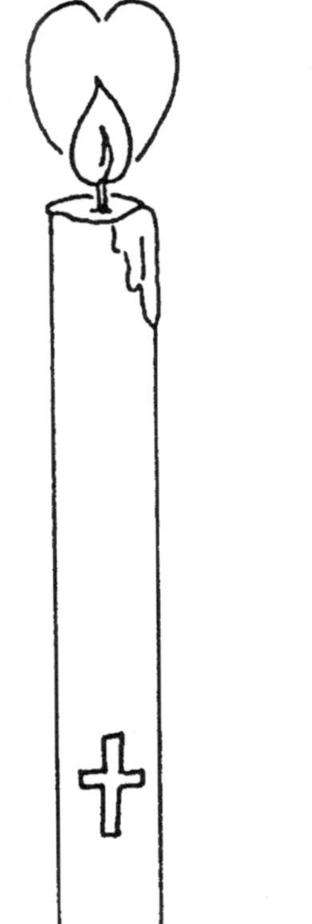

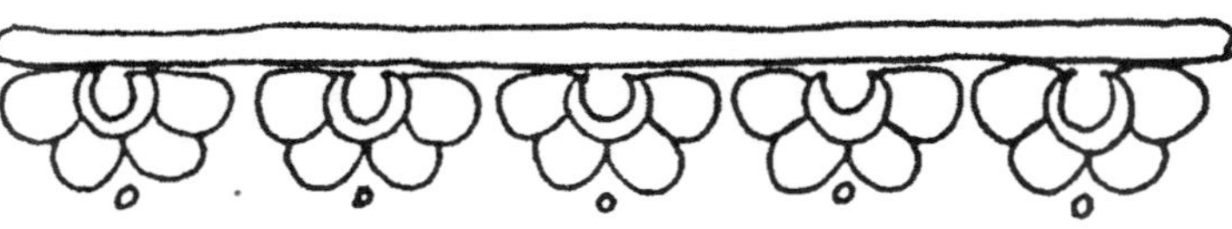

*Congratulations, you are a godparent!*

# Remembering Baptism

_______________________ and _______________________

**are chosen to be
the godparents
of**

_________________________________________________

**Born on**

_________________________________________________

**and celebrated Baptism on**

_________________________________________________

_________________________________________________
*Priest or Deacon*

_________________________________________________
*Parish*                                    *Mother*

_________________________________________________
*City, State*                               *Father*

Dear Godparent,

The role of a godparent is an honor and privilege but also a great responsibility. You are being asked to invite this family and child into your life and to share the task of handing on the faith. Offer your support and help in the Catholic formation of your godchild. Be a source of guidance and inspiration as this child grows in faith. God's love will be reflected through your actions, appreciation, and care for the child.

There are many things that you may do to nurture your relationship with your godchild as you share a life of faith. Live a life that reflects your faith both in words and actions. Talk to your godchild about God and your faith. As your godchild grows share and discuss your Christian values. Serve as a compassionate guide through prayer and conversation.

Celebrate the anniversary of the Baptism each year. Share memories and pictures of the day. Light the baptismal candle and say prayers of thanksgiving for this treasured child. If you are not able to be there send a card or call your godchild to mark this special day.

Remember your godchild on special days or important events in your godchild's life such as Christmas, Easter, birthdays, the first day of school, and graduations. Send a card with a note or give a gift that will reflect your godchild's growing faith: a nativity set, advent calendar, Bible, prayer book, religious jewelry, a book on the saints, or age-appropriate Bible story books.

# Record of Baptism

Child of _______________________________
name of parents

born on the _______ day of ___________
month          year

in _________________________________
city                    state

was Baptized

_______________________________________
child's name

in the name of
the Father, Son and Holy Spirit

on the ___________ day of ___________
month          year

by _________________________________
priest/deacon

at the Catholic Church

of ___________________________

located in ___________________________
city                    state

Godparents ___________________________

_______________________________________

Baptism certificate
- copy on a heavy stock paper
- use information received on baptism information sheet to fill in the blanks

# Bulletin announcements

*Bulletin announcements of the parish Baptisms will keep the community well informed.*

- Routinely make the community aware of the Baptism preparation sessions being offered so that this step is not unexpected for families planning to have a child baptized.
- At least one week before, invite the community to participate in the sacrament by publishing the dates and times of upcoming Baptism celebrations.
- Encourage the community to offer support to the families of the newly baptized.

Adapt the following examples to fit the needs of your parish:

## Baptism preparation sessions for parents

*"I will sprinkle clean water upon you to cleanse you from all your impurities … I will give you a new heart and place a new spirit within you"* (Ezekiel 36:25-26).

The Baptism of your child is truly something to celebrate! Baptism preparation sessions will be offered on (date) at (time) in the church for all parents who are interested in having their child baptized. Please call the parish office (phone #) to register. The sessions are meant to help parents prepare for and celebrate the Baptism of their child in a joyful and meaningful way.

## A celebration of Baptism

*"As a body is one though it has many parts, and are the parts of the body, though many, are one body, so also Christ"* (1 Corinthians 12:12).

The sacrament of Baptism will be celebrated in our community on (date) at (time). All members of (parish's name) are welcome as we celebrate the lives of these children, their new life in Christ and in our community.

## Welcome into the Catholic community

*There is but "one Lord, one faith, one baptism, one God and Father of all"* (Ephesians 4:5-6).

Congratulations! This weekend we welcome the following children into the Catholic community of faith:

(date and time)
(child's name), son of (parents' names)

(date and time)
(child's name), daughter of (parents' names)

May our community embrace these children and may our word and example be a reflection of God's love for them. Let us offer our joy-filled prayers and congratulations as a sign of our support and welcome!

# Tips for group discussion

**• Offer a climate of welcome and openness**

The people who come to Baptism preparation will be from various walks of life.  Each person will bring his/her own set of values, beliefs, and attitudes.  Be sensitive to the non-Catholic spouses and single parents who may be hesitant about their participation in the sessions.  Accept and respect people for who they are and where they are coming from.

**• Encourage and affirm group members**

 Some people are very shy and have a difficult time sharing their thoughts and feelings.  Other members of your group may be uncomfortable sharing their faith or with the community prayer.  Be sensitive and responsive to their insights and faith experiences that are shared.

**• Keep things on track**

It is very easy to get off track with a group, especially if you have a very talkative or opinionated member.  If one member of the group is dominating the discussion, gently bring the group back by thanking that person for his/her comments and asking others for their input.  If the entire group is off track, redirect the group with a new question.

**• Count on the Holy Spirit**

Be assured of the Holy Spirit's presence. Remember that the Holy Spirit moves and works in wondrous ways!

**• Listen carefully**

People will be much more open if they think you are listening and care about what they have to say.  Use good eye contact and positive facial expressions to show your attentiveness.

**• Relax and enjoy what you are doing**

The key is to simply relax and enjoy the group and discussion.  Your attitude and openness will help to set the tone of the discussion.

---

# Presentation guide

A few simple steps to leading a great presentation:

*Read the provided outline several times.*  Highlight ideas that you consider to be the main points.

*Organize the material in a manner that you are comfortable with.*

*Make an outline of your own,* adding an appropriate story, illustration, or reference to a common human experience.

*Consider using visual aids.* Use an overhead projector, a chalkboard, a dry mark board, or newsprint to jot down key words or phrases during your talk.  Remember to keep them simple and visible to everyone.

End with one of the following:
• Summary of points
• Story
• Quotation

*Practice the presentation until you feel comfortable with it.*

*Shake off the butterflies with preparation and organization.* Concentrate on the message of your presentation.

*Remember as you speak to:*
• Maintain eye contact
• Speak slowly
• Use vocal variety
• Use expressive gestures

# *Assembling Baptism candle kits*

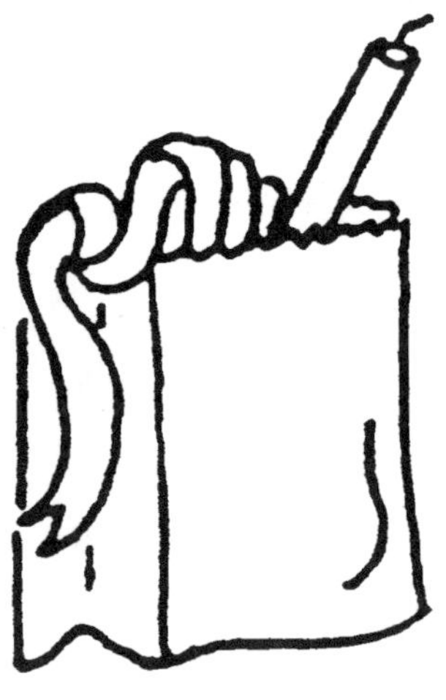

If the desire of the parish is to have a uniform candle for each child being baptized, do one of the following:

• Provide the basic materials needed with specific instructions on assembling the candle (see page 41) OR
• Incorporate the candle decorating into the session two process, providing the needed materials and instruction on how to assemble the candle.

If the desire is for the families to select their own baptismal candle and method:

• Provide a very basic kit and offer suggestions on how to assemble (see page 41)
OR
• Provide suggestions as to where a candle might be purchased.

Suggested basic candle kit:
• White candle
• 3x3-inch squares of silver or gold metallic contact paper
• 10-12-inch pieces of satin or metallic ribbon
Suggested colors: light blue, red, white, silver or gold

Helpful tips for packing the kits:
• Pack materials in white paper bags.
• Involve other members of the parish:
　Have children in religious education classes decorate the white paper bags with symbols of Baptism.
　Invite parent groups to pack the kits and add a note of welcome.

# *How to prepare a parish information insert*

*(Note: If the parish has a brochure that explains the various existing ministries and organizations offered in the parish community, use it to replace this insert.)*

**Collect basic facts**

Invite parish associations to supply the following information for their organization or ministry:
* Name of the association's contact person
* Phone number of contact person
* Association's meeting dates and times

Give the leadership of these groups a self-addressed, stamped postcard in which they only

Dear Parish Leadership,
   To help us better inform parents in the Baptism preparation sessions of the many groups open to their participation, please provide the following details about your organization for us to share.

Group's name: ______________________________
Contact person: ______________________________
Phone number: ______________________________
Dates and times the group meets: ______________
Group's purpose: ______________________________

need to fill in the requested details and mail back to you.

**Create insert**

Use the example (see page 63) as a guide to create an insert with the collected information that describes how to become involved with the various organizations of the parish.

**Circulate information**

Distribute the insert at the Baptism preparation sessions as parish participation is discussed.

**front**

**Weekend Mass Schedule**
Saturday .............................................. 4:30 p.m.
Sunday ............ 8:00 a.m.; 9:30 a.m.; 11:00 a.m.

**Family Fun**
call Mary and Paul Fritz
for upcoming events ............................ 555-1212

**Women's Spirituality**
Helen Knight ........................................ 555-4637

**Sunday Nursery**
Cindy Gleason ..................................... 555-1495

**Faith Formation Ministries**
Preschool-Adult
Jackie Joncas, director ........................ 555-0677

**back**

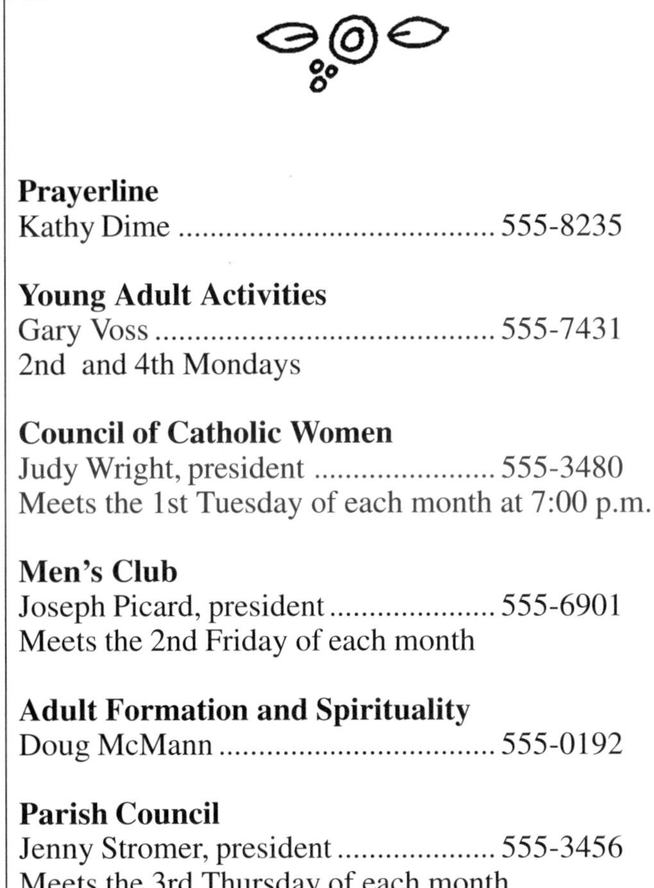

**Prayerline**
Kathy Dime ......................................... 555-8235

**Young Adult Activities**
Gary Voss ............................................ 555-7431
2nd  and 4th Mondays

**Council of Catholic Women**
Judy Wright, president ...................... 555-3480
Meets the 1st Tuesday of each month at 7:00 p.m.

**Men's Club**
Joseph Picard, president ..................... 555-6901
Meets the 2nd Friday of each month

**Adult Formation and Spirituality**
Doug McMann .................................... 555-0192

**Parish Council**
Jenny Stromer, president .................... 555-3456
Meets the 3rd Thursday of each month

# Bibliography


## Church Documents

*The Catechism of the Catholic Church*, Congregation for the Doctrine of the Faith (Washington, D.C.: United States Catholic Conference, 1994).

*The Documents of Vatican II*, Abbott and Gallagher, editor. (Boston:The American Press, 1966).

*A Family Perspective in Church and Society* (Washington, D.C.: United States Catholic Conference, 1981).

Pope John Paul II, **Familiaris Consortio**, *Apostolic Exhortation on the Family* (Washington, D.C.: United States Catholic Conference, 1981).

National Catechetical Directory for Catholics of the United States, *Sharing the Light of Faith* (Washington, D.C.: United States Catholic Conference, 1979).

*The Rite of Baptism for Children* (Washington, D.C.: International Committee on English in the Liturgy, Inc., 1969).

## Other Resources

Robert J. Baker, Larry J. Nyberg and Victoria M. Tufano, editors, *A Baptism Sourcebook* (Chicago: Liturgy Training Press, 1993).

Sandra DiGidiio, *RCIA: The Rites Revisited* (Minneapolis: Winston Press, 1984).

Timothy Fitzgerald, *Infant Baptism: A Parish Celebration* (Chicago: Liturgy Training Press, 1994).

Gabe Huck, editor, *The Liturgy Documents: A Parish Resource* (Chicago: Liturgy Training Press, 1980).

Adian Kavanagh, *The Shape of Baptism: The Rite of Christian Initiation* (New York: Pueblo Publishing Company, 1978).

Alfred McBride, O. Praem., *Essentials of the Faith: A Guide to the Catechism of the Catholic Church* (Huntington, Ind.: Our Sunday Visitor, 1994).

Gertrud Mueller Nelson, *To Dance with God: Family Ritual and Community Celebration* (New York: Paulist Press, 1986).

Kenan B. Osborne, *The Christian Sacraments of Initiation: Baptism, Confirmation, Eucharist* (New York: Paulist Press, 1987).

Elaine Ramshaw, *The Godparent Book* (Chicago: Liturgy Training Press, 1993).

Mark Searle, *Christening: The Making of Christians* (Collegeville, Minn.: Liturgical Press, 1980).

Mary Ann Simcoe, editor, *The Liturgy Documents* (Chicago: Liturgy Training Publications, 1985).

James A. Wilde, *Finding and Forming Sponsors and Godparents* (Chicago: Liturgy Training Publications, 1988).